New Vanguard • 125

Huey Cobra Gunships

Chris Bishop · Illustrated by Jim Laurier

First published in Great Britain in 2006 by Osprey Publishing, Midland House, West Way, Botley, Oxford OX2 0PH, UK
443 Park Avenue South, New York, NY 10016, USA
E-mail: info@ospreypublishing.com

A CIP catalog record for this book is available from the British Library

ISBN-10: 1 84176 984 3
ISBN-13: 978 1 84176 984 4

Page layout by Ken Vail Graphic Design, Cambridge, UK
Index by Alison Worthington
Typeset in Helvetica Neue and ITC New Baskerville
Originated by United Graphics Pte Ltd, Singapore
Printed in China through Worldprint Ltd

06 07 08 09 10   10 9 8 7 6 5 4 3 2 1

For a catalog of all books published by Osprey Military and Aviation please contact:

NORTH AMERICA
Osprey Direct, c/o Random House Distribution Center, 400 Hahn Road, Westminster, MD 21157
E-mail: info@ospreydirect.com

ALL OTHER REGIONS
Osprey Direct UK, P.O. Box 140 Wellingborough, Northants, NN8 2FA, UK
E-mail: info@ospreydirect.co.uk

www.ospreypublishing.com

Artist's note

Readers may care to note that prints of the digital artwork from which the color plates in this book were prepared are available for private sale. All reproduction copyright whatsoever is retained by the Publishers. All inquiries should be addressed to:

Jim Laurier, 85 Carroll Street, Keene, New Hampshire, NH 03431, USA

The Publishers regret that they can enter into no correspondence upon this matter.

Glossary

AAFSS – Advanced Aerial Fire Support System
ARA – Aerial Rocket Artillery
CCM – Canopy/Cockpit Modification
C-NITE – Cobra Night Attack
FAE – Fuel-air explosive
FARP – Forward Air Refueling Point
FFAR – Folding Fin Aerial Rocket
FLIR – Forward-looking Infrared
GPS – Global Positioning Satellite
HUD – Head-up display
IRCM – Infrared Countermeasures
LLTV – Low Light TV
NOE – "Nap of the Earth" operations
NTS – Night Targeting System
SMS – Stabilized Multisensor Sight
TSU – Telescopic Sight Unit
TOW – Tube-launched, Optically tracked, Wire-guided missile
TSS – Target Sight System

HUEY COBRA GUNSHIPS

INTRODUCTION

They called it the "Snake," Fast, slender, and lethal, the Bell AH-1 Cobra was the first true helicopter gunship, which entered service in Vietnam in the 1960s as an interim weapons platform for the US Army. It would only serve, it was thought, until a new purpose-designed gunship became operational in the early 1970s. Nearly four decades later, that interim solution is still in frontline service all over the world and is a success story beyond the wildest dreams of its earliest users.

The Cobra traces its lineage from the Bell UH-1 Huey. The original Cobra retained the Huey's engine, transmission, and other major parts, but replaced the Huey's bulky fuselage with a thin-profile fuselage with tandem seating. The US Marine Corps (USMC) later adopted a twin-engine variant of the airframe to perform troop helicopter escort.

Through the years, the Cobra has gone through extensive modernization. The AH-1F Cobra, with its proven firepower and maneuverability, went on to fight in every major US military operation since Vietnam until it was retired by the US Army at the end of the 1990s. The current AH-1 Super Cobra has also evolved considerably. Today's US Marine Corps AH-1W boasts an advanced Night Targeting System (NTS) and a full suite of advanced weaponry and countermeasures. Still a two-seater, the Super Cobra is now a twin-engine attack helicopter operating from land bases or ships. The rear-seat pilot usually controls the aircraft in flight, while the gunner in the front cockpit handles the aircraft's weapons systems (although he also has a full set of aircraft controls).

In service for nearly four decades, the Bell AH-1 Huey Cobra is still a potent frontline weapon system in the 21st century. The AH-1Z, the ultimate successor to the original single-engine, daylight-only Cobra, is a twin-engine multirole machine able to engage and destroy targets by day or night on land, at sea and in the air. (US Navy Systems Command)

The Cobra still provides the rotary-winged close support of troops on the ground for which it was designed, but it can also fly antiarmor and anti-helicopter missions, as well as providing armed escort, and armed and visual reconnaissance capabilities by day or by night. Other missions flown by this multirole machine include anti-shipping operations, and the coordination and forward control of fixed-wing attack aircraft, artillery, infantry support weapons, and naval gunfire. It was one of the first attack helicopters that could use air-to-air and anti-radar missiles in combat.

ORIGINS AND DEVELOPMENT

Armed helicopters were first proposed in the 1950s, and after their combat debut with the British in Malaya and the French in Algeria they came into widespread use in Vietnam in the early 1960s. The first armed helicopters were modified variants of utility helicopters, equipped with strap-on weapons packs. Early piston-engined helicopters, however, lacked the reserves of power needed to carry heavy weapons loads, and their marginal performance made them vulnerable to ground fire. The first successful gunships were based on the turbine-powered Huey.

As the US Army's involvement in Vietnam grew through the early 1960s, Bell's UH-1 Iroquois or Huey, first flown in 1956, became the workhorse of Army rotary-winged combat operations. The UH-1A was originally deployed to Southeast Asia as a medevac helicopter in 1962, but armed versions were soon being improvised as the Huey became the Army's first operational helicopter gunship.

The UH-1A was underpowered, but it was followed by the bigger and more powerful UH-1B and the still more powerful UH-1C. However, combat experience demonstrated that the Huey left something to be desired in the helicopter gunship role. It was still too slow and vulnerable.

What was needed was a light, fast, armed escort helicopter designed specifically to carry weapons and be able to target them very accurately. Plans for such an aircraft had in fact been set into motion long before US troops arrived in Vietnam. The Bell Helicopter company, which had been taken over by Textron in 1960, had been looking at the idea of a dedicated helicopter gunship since the late 1950s. It unveiled a mockup of such a helicopter in June 1962.

Based on the powerplant, transmission, and rotor system of the Huey, the "Iroquois Warrior" had a completely new fuselage. Long, slender, with the appearance of a fighter, it introduced the classic gunship configuration that has since been followed by almost every aircraft of this type. The tandem two-seat cockpit housed a gunner in front and a pilot in the back, with the rear seat stepped up to give the pilot forward visibility.

The Warrior was to be equipped with a chin turret housing an automatic grenade launcher. Further planned armament included a 20mm cannon in a belly pack and stub wings with stores pylons to carry a variety of munitions, including rockets and SS-11 antitank missiles.

The Army, by now operating with inadequate machines in Southeast Asia, thought that the idea was worth following. It awarded Bell a proof-of-concept contract in December 1962. Bell quickly produced the Model 207 Sioux Scout, which was completed in August 1963, and was based on the company's long-established piston-powered Model 47, in service as the OH-13 Sioux. The Sioux Scout featured a streamlined fuselage with a tandem cockpit and a chin turret mounting a pair of 7.62mm M60 machine guns. Too light for real operational use, it was purely a demonstration machine, bearing only a general similarity to the Iroquois Warrior mockup. However, it was enough to give the Army an idea of what a dedicated gunship should be like.

Army tacticians decided that they needed an operational gunship, but they wanted something far more sophisticated than the Sioux Scout, or even the Iroquois Warrior. In August 1964 they announced a requirement for an Advanced Aerial Fire Support System (AAFSS), and set up a competition for the design. Several companies submitted proposals, and the Army selected the most advanced design, the Lockheed AH-56 Cheyenne, as being the most likely to meet its needs. Roll-out of the first prototype was on May 3, 1967. Unfortunately, production Cheyennes were not likely to be available until the early 1970s. To fill the gap, the Army asked for proposals for an interim gunship design, the Agile Attack Helicopter or AAH. To save time, it was to be based on an existing helicopter, and was to be equipped with a simpler fire-control and navigation system than the AH-56A. Proposed airplanes varied greatly in size and capability, from a modified Chinook suggested by Boeing-Vertol to a modified Kaman Sea Sprite and a re-modeled UH-1 from Bell.

Bell had been thinking about gunships since the late 1950s. Their first flying prototype, the Model 207 Sioux Scout, displayed many of the features that have since become standard on such machines. It had a slim, tandem-cockpit fuselage, stub wings, and a chin-mounted gun armament. (Bell Helicopter)

Bell had a head start on its rivals. Eliminated from the AAFSS program in the early stages of the competition, the company had funded its own development of a dedicated helicopter gunship. They called the new design the Model 209. While it shared many parts with the UH-1, it was in effect a new helicopter. Bell managed to persuade Army officials that its radically different appearance would not delay development of a production aircraft, and the Army accepted the company's assurances.

The Model 209 demonstrator strongly resembled the Iroquois Warrior. It featured a similar snakelike fuselage, with tandem seats and stub wings. The engine, an Avco Lycoming T53-L-11 turboshaft engine delivering 1,100hp (820kW) was taken directly from the UH-1C Huey, as was the rotor system (featuring an electromechanical Stability Control Augmentation System – SCAS – in place of the traditional Bell crosswise stabilizing bar) and the entire tail boom assembly.

The Model 209 was armed with an Emerson Electric chin turret mounting a 7.62mm General Electric GAU-2B/A six-barreled Minigun. The stub wings could mount four stores pylons. These could carry rocket pods that fired folding-fin air-to-ground rockets, gun pods, or other stores. The Model 209 demonstrator was fitted with a retractable skid undercarriage, more to improve the field of fire of the chin-mounted gun than for aerodynamic performance.

Bell proposed the Model 209 to the Army in August 1965, and the new helicopter made its first flight a month later, on September 7, 1965. In October, it set a world helicopter speed record for its class of 172 knots (200mph). In November 1965, the Army carried out a series of trials in which the competing designs were tested against each other. The Model 209 was declared the winner, and on April 7, 1966, a contract was placed with Bell for two operational prototypes, followed six days later by a production contract for 110 helicopter gunships. The production Model 209 was originally designated UH-1H, but in July 1966 the designation was changed to AH-1.

Traditionally, Army aircraft have been named after Native American tribes. However, when the AH-1 was ordered the Department of Defense was engaged in a legal battle with Piper Aircraft, which also used tribal names for its aircraft, so a different type of name was needed.

UH-1 Hueys operating in Vietnam at the time were known as "Slicks" if they were unarmed transports, "Hogs" if they carried rockets, and "Cobras" if they were armed with guns. To maintain the threadbare idea that the

Clearly based on the lessons learned with the Model 207, the prototype of the Model 209 was an altogether more elegant-looking machine. It was based on the mechanical components of the UH-1C Iroquois, which were mated to a slim, snakelike fuselage. (Bell Helicopter)

AH-1 was really just a modified Huey, it was decided to name the new gunship Huey Cobra.

The decision to buy the Cobra was not without its opponents in the Army hierarchy. Those most heavily involved in the development of the AH-56A Cheyenne resented the diversion of resources and finance, even though the Cobra's extensive use of Huey components made it a good economic proposition. Those at the sharp end, the operators, needed a workable weapons system as soon as possible.

It was the director of Army Aviation, Colonel George P. Seneff, who settled the issue. When asked what the soldiers in Vietnam needed, Seneff told generals Harold K. Johnson and Creighton Abrams, respectively Army Chief of Staff and Deputy Chief of Staff, that soldiers in Southeast Asia were dying now, not in the future. They needed the Cobra, not some all-singing, all-dancing machine that might not be available for years. Ultimately the Department of Defense contracted with Bell Helicopters for 1,100 AH-1s, which logged more than 1 million flight hours in Vietnam.

For the next six years the Model 209 demonstrator was used as a trials machine, testing various weapons and equipment fits. By the early 1970s it had been modified to production AH-1 standard. However, when it was retired to the Patton Museum at Fort Knox, Kentucky, it was returned to an approximation of its original appearance.

The AH-1 Huey Cobra prototype flies in formation with a UH-1B and a UH-1D. With its smaller and lighter fuselage, the gunship was much faster than its utility half-brothers, and could stay on station in a combat zone for much longer. (Bell Helicopter)

VARIANTS

Production Cobras differed from the demonstrator in a number of ways. Carried over from the original Model 209 were the slim fuselage with tandem cockpits, the Lycoming T-53 engine, the two stores stations under each stub wing, and the chin turret. The retractable skids were a needless complication, and they were replaced by fixed skids on production machines. The first production variant, the AH-1G, featured a new wide-blade rotor, and coupled with its slim, lightweight fuselage it made the Cobra twice as fast as the UH-1B Huey. It could also loiter over a target area more than three times as long as the overloaded gunship versions of the UH-1.

The AH-1G was the baseline for subsequent members of the family. For lightness and strength, the fuselage was built of an aluminum honeycomb, with access panels for easy maintenance. The 247 US gallon (936 liter) fuel tank was self-sealing, and further protection was provided by light armor over the engine, fuel systems, and hydraulic systems.

The crew members were also protected by armored seats with side panels that could be pulled up for extra protection. The gunner was further shielded by an armored plate in the nose. However, the canopy was standard Plexiglas; the armored glass fitted to the Model 209 demonstrator was so heavy it would have affected performance.

The GAU-2B/A Minigun in the TAT-102A turret was fed by 8,000 rounds of ammunition. However, the Minigun turret was always considered

The first production variant of the Cobra was the AH-1G. Its primary armament was provided by 2.75in folding-fin rockets, originally used in the 1950s as unguided air-to-air missiles but which had been adapted to devastating effect as ground-attack weapons. (US Army)

an interim feature, and it was soon replaced by the TAT-141 turret armed either with two Miniguns with 4,000 rounds each, or a single Minigun and an M129 40mm grenade launcher with between 200 and 300 (some sources say 231) rounds of ammunition. The Minigun could fire at two rates: low rate of 2,000 rounds per minute (rpm) or high rate of 4,000rpm. The grenade launcher had a maximum rate of fire of 450rpm. The turret could be aimed 25 degrees upward, 60 degrees downward, and through over 230 degrees of arc. Although the gunner normally operated the turret, the pilot could also fire it in the fixed-forward position in an emergency. The gunner also had simple flight controls to allow him to fly the machine if anything happened to the pilot.

Most of the time the AH-1G also carried 2.75in Folding Fin Aerial Rockets (FFARs) in seven-tube M158 or 19-tube M200 rocket launchers. These were used by Aerial Rocket Artillery (ARA) units, which provided devastating fire support to ground troops. The AH-1G could also be armed with the M134 Minigun in fixed M18 gun pods. The port side mounting could carry the M195 20mm cannon as part of the M35 armament subsystem.

The AH-1G Cobra was first deployed to Vietnam in September 1967. The Cobra's primary mission was to escort troop-carrying Hueys and to provide them with fire support. Its introduction to service equipped ground commanders with immediately available integral fire support that could be provided much more quickly than by calling on Air Force close support assets. Additionally, the Cobra's narrow fuselage – only 38in (96.5cm) wide – presented the enemy with a much more difficult target than the larger UH-1 Huey gunships. During the conflict, the Cobra was used in a variety of missions ranging from armed escort and reconnaissance to fire suppression and aerial rocket artillery.

TOW Cobras

During the early 1970s, the threat posed by the huge number of Soviet and Warsaw Pact tanks in Eastern Europe was of great concern to NATO planners. The AH-56 Cheyenne had been intended to counter the Soviet threat, and ten prototypes had been completed by 1972. However, the program was terminated on August 9, 1972, due to technical problems that had delayed development and to soaring program costs. The Cheyenne's mission would eventually be covered by the Army's Advanced Attack Helicopter (AAH) which would finally emerge in the shape of the Hughes (later McDonnell Douglas and currently Boeing) AH-64 Apache.

The cancellation of the Cheyenne left NATO with a major capability gap that would possibly last for a decade or more. In an attempt to counter the threat from the east, the US Army conducted a series of tests to determine the suitability of the AH-1G Cobra as an antiarmor platform. Taking place in Ansbach, Germany, the tests showed that helicopter-mounted tank hunters could destroy large numbers of enemy armored vehicles for every missile-firing helicopter lost.

Although helicopters are inherently vulnerable to ground fire in high-threat environments, it was shown that teams of armed scout and attack helicopters operating at night or at very low level could survive and even thrive in high-intensity warfare.

AH-1Q

In March 1972, the Army requested that Bell develop a system for arming the AH-1G with the TOW missile under the Improved Cobra Armament Program or ICAP. TOW stands for Tube-launched, Optically tracked, Wire-guided. On launch, the TOW missile trails out wires that keep it in communication with the launch platform. The missile has two infrared flares on

its tail that are tracked by the Stabilized Multisensor Sight (SMS). All the gunner has to do is keep the target in his sight, and the missile fire-control system adjusts its flight appropriately.

Bell equipped eight AH-1Gs with the new Bell-Hughes XM26 Telescopic Sight Unit (TSU) in the nose, and two M56 four-pack TOW launchers, with one launcher fitted to the outboard pylon on each stub wing. M200 19-tube 2.75in rocket launchers could be carried on the inboard pylons.

These eight Cobras were redesignated YAH-1Q, and over the two years from early 1973 they performed a long series of TOW test firings. The Army was satisfied that the YAH-1Q met its short-term needs, and ordered the conversion of 101 AH-1Gs to the production AH-1Q configuration, featuring the M56 TOW launchers, the M65 production version of the M26 TSU, and Sperry-Univac helmet-mounted sights. The first AH-1Q was delivered to the Army in early 1975 and became known as the TOW Cobra.

Even before the first AH-1Qs were operational, however, it was recognized that they lacked the power to carry a heavy load of TOW missiles and still be able to perform demanding maneuvers at an extremely low level, flying at or even below treetop height in what became known as "Nap of the Earth" or NOE operations. In 1975 the Army established the Improved Cobra Agility and Maneuverability (ICAM) program to address this problem.

Bell fitted an AH-1G with an uprated Lycoming T53-L-703 turboshaft delivering 1,800hp (1,323kW) through a new and improved drivetrain. The resulting aircraft was redesignated as the YAH-1R, while a similar modification to an AH-1Q airframe was given the designation YAH-1S. The new engine gave the Cobra enough power to handle a full TOW missile load, and the Army ordered conversion of all 92 surviving AH-1Qs, plus 198 AH-1Gs, to the new configuration known as the AH-1S.

AH-1S

The original designation of Modified AH-1S referred to all existing AH-1G/AH-1Q Cobras upgraded to Production AH-1S standard from 1976 onward. The addition of the TOW missile system meant that the Cobra's primary mission was now to destroy tanks, but the type retained its original direct fire support, armed escort, and reconnaissance capabilities.

The Modified AH-1S could be identified by the snub-nosed mounting for the TSU. The AH-1S also had the original rounded crew canopy

From the start, the possibility of arming the AH-1 with antitank missiles was recognized. This early AH-1G, seen in the mid-1960s, is taking part in trials of the Rockwell AGM-64 Viper missile, which was to evolve into the highly successful laser-guided AGM-114 Hellfire. (US Army via Aerospace/Art-Tech)

instead of the flat-panel canopy that was to become standard with the new production AH-1S. Some AH-1S Cobras received the Cobra Night Attack or C-NITE upgrade, which allowed the gunner to designate and acquire targets during night-time or adverse weather operating conditions.

AH-1P

The original AH-1S marked the beginning of a series of refinements or "Steps" which were applied to the TOW Cobra family. The Step 1 variant was the new-build Production AH-1S or AH-1S(PROD), which was redesignated AH-1P in 1988. One hundred AH-1P TOW Cobras were built and delivered to the Army in 1977 and 1978. They featured an even more powerful engine system, as well as the distinctive new flat-plate canopy characteristic of late-model Army Cobras. Although the new canopy gave the Cobra a more aggressive look, the change was made primarily to improve visibility by reducing the glint off the window glass, and therefore it did not include armored glass.

The AH-1P also featured an improved T-shaped instrument and control panel layout to make NOE flight simpler for the pilot, along with a radar altimeter and improved radios, a radar warning receiver, and, from the 67th production unit onward, Kaman K-747 composite rotor blades with tapered tips. The K-747 rotor blades were also retrofitted to older Cobra variants. Some of the gunships were temporarily refitted with metal blades in the mid-1980s, when a few K-747 composite blades lost their tips due to bonding problems, but this issue was quickly resolved.

The AH-1P version of the Cobra was first fielded by the 82d Airborne Division at Fort Bragg, North Carolina, in August 1977.

AH-1E

The Step 2 variant was variously known as the Up-Gun AH-1S, AH-1S Enhanced Cobra Armament System, or AH-1S(ECAS), but was redesignated as AH-1E in 1988. All Army Cobra variants to this time had been equipped with the original Cobra's TAT-141 turret, but the AH-1E featured a much more powerful gun armament in the shape of the three-barrel

20mm M197 cannon and universal turret introduced on the Marine Corps' AH-1J. The AH-1E retained the M65 TOW/Cobra missile system, but since the new variant lacked a rocket management system it could not operate with the 2.75in FFAR rockets used by all other Cobras. However, the ECAS incorporated automatic compensation for off-axis gun firing. Ninety-eight new-build AH-1Es were delivered in 1978 and 1979.

AH-1F

The Step 3 variant was originally designated as the Modernized AH-1S, the AH-1S Modernized Cobra, or the AH-1S(MC), but was renamed the AH-1F when Cobra designations were rationalized in 1988. It was the US Army's final operational standard for the Cobra gunship.

A total of 530 AH-1Fs were produced: 387 were converted from old AH-1G airframes (including 41 dual-control TAH-1F trainers) and 143 were new production aircraft. Fifty were built for the US Army National Guard (ANG) through to 1986, when the last new-build single-engine Cobra for US forces was completed. At that time, the US Army had 1,100 Cobras in its inventory.

The AH-1F featured all the improvements of the AH-1P and the AH-1E, along with numerous refinements: a new fire-control system with a laser rangefinder; a new computer; secure voice communications; an M76 head-up display (HUD) for the pilot; an AN/ALQ-144 Infrared Countermeasures (IRCM) unit mounted above the engine; a cable cutter above and below the cockpit to protect the Cobra in NOE flight; and a long exhaust pipe to reduce the helicopter's infrared signature. The AH-1F had a distinctive blister at the front of the rotor transmission system housing for a laser tracker, but this was never fitted. Externally it differed from other modernized AH-1S variants only in the fitting of a new air data sensor mounted above the right side of the canopy.

The M147 Rocket Management Subsystem (RMS) meant that the AH-1F regained the ability to use the standard 2.75in rocket system, in addition to the M65 TOW/Cobra missile system and the M197 20mm gun. Typically, these rockets were fired from seven-tube M158, 19-tube M200, seven-tube M260, or 19-tube M261 rocket pods. Some AH-1F Cobras were fitted with the C-NITE upgrade. The threat from shoulder-launched heat-seeking surface-to-air missiles meant that countermeasures became essential equipment. The AH-1S and its derivatives were equipped with an infrared jammer mounted on the top of the engine fairing and an extended exhaust nozzle that suppressed infrared radiation as a counter to heat-seeking missiles. Additionally, most could be fitted with the M130 flare and chaff dispenser.

All modernized Cobras, including the AH-1S, AH-1P, and AH-1E used the M73 reflex sight for optical sighting and fire control and were equipped with the TSU. None of the four armament subsystems used with the four AH-1S variants were interchangeable without considerable modification or conversion.

By the early 1980s, TOW Cobras were in service with frontline units in Germany, where they served alongside the newly introduced M1 Abrams main battle tank. This shot was taken during one of the massive REFORGER exercises, in which NATO practiced reinforcing Germany in time of war. (US Army)

The AH-1F was the focus of a series of small and fairly minor updates, including being given the ability to fire Stinger air-to-air missiles. However, in spite of these improvements, the single-engine Cobra was becoming increasingly outdated. In 1999 it was phased out of regular US Army combat service when the 25th Infantry Division (Light) decommissioned the type in a ceremony in Hawaii, replacing the Cobras with OH-58D Kiowa Warriors. The division's old aircraft were transferred to the ANG, which continued to use the type but in rapidly declining numbers.

Under the Army's 2000 Aviation Force Modernization Plan, Cobras and Kiowas were to be replaced by AH-64D Apaches and eventually by RAH-66 Comanches, the new reconnaissance and attack helicopter which had been scheduled to enter service in 2008, but which was cancelled in 2004.

Marine Cobras: The AH-1J

The Marines also operated armed Hueys in Vietnam, and were quick to see the value of the Huey Cobra. They initially acquired 38 AH-1Gs drawn from Army stocks. However, unlike Army aircraft, Marine gunships could be expected to fly long over-water missions, and they considered the single-engine AH-1G to have inadequate safety reserve in such conditions. As a result, the Corps looked to order its own version of the Cobra in May 1968.

The Marine requirement called for an AH-1G with two engines; this led to the development of the AH-1J Sea Cobra. This was powered by the Pratt & Whitney Twinpac T400 engine, which was, in effect, two 900hp (662kW) turboshaft engines coupled together. Total output power of the engine system was 1,530hp (1,125kW), compared to the 1,400hp (1,029kW) of the AH-1G's Lycoming T53-L-13 engine. The Twinpac engine was actually capable of providing 1,800hp (1,323kW), but the helicopter's drivetrain was not strong enough to support it and when both engines were running they were power-limited. When one went out, the other could be run at full power.

At first, the Department of Defense opposed the order in the belief that commonality with Army AH-1Gs outweighed the advantages of a different engine fit. However, the Marine view prevailed, and Bell was awarded a contract for 49 twin-engine AH-1Js in May 1968. The first AH-1J made its initial flight in November 1969.

Additionally, Marine Cobras also received an increase in strike power with the installation of a new turret equipped with the three-barrel XM197 20mm cannon. This was a three-barrel version of the six-barrel

M61 Vulcan cannon, and would eventually become the standard turret weapon for both Marine and Army Cobras. The M197 had a rate of fire of 750rpm, though it could only fire 16-round bursts, and the AH-1J carried a supply of 750 rounds.

The Marines bought a second batch of AH-1Js, bringing total procurement to 69, with the last rolled out in February 1975. The AH-1J and later twin-engine Huey Cobra variants are sometimes referred to as Twin Cobras.

The Marines depend on attack helicopters to provide pinpoint close-in fire support in amphibious operations. They are also vital in providing support to ground troops, who often engage the enemy beyond the range of conventional artillery. Marine AH-1s are tasked with a wide variety of other missions, including landing-zone fire-suppression support; armed escort for helicopters carrying troops or cargo; convoy escort and fire suppression; visual armed reconnaissance; forward air control (fighter direction and target marking); and antiarmor operations. They are expected to operate from ships or land bases, and over the last decade have added the ability to provide air-to-air defense of other helicopters against enemy gunships.

While recognizably still a Cobra, the AH-1J Sea Cobra developed for the US Marine Corps was a more powerful machine, optimized for use in a maritime environment and with twin-engine power for increased reliability on long over-water operations. (US Marine Corps via Aerospace/Art-Tech)

Model 309 King Cobra

From the start of the Cobra program, the US Army considered the AH-1G as an interim solution to its gunship requirement. It had been a success as a "Jungle Fighter" in Southeast Asia, but the Army's broader concern was the task of protecting Western Europe. Following the end of World War II, Europe had been divided between the former Allied powers, and rivalry between the capitalist West and the communist East quickly developed a military dimension.

An "Iron Curtain" had descended over the center of the continent, and two great military alliances emerged facing each other in what became known as the Cold War. NATO, led by the United States, was primarily a defensive alliance, dedicated to stopping the Soviet-dominated Warsaw Pact from rolling over the democratic nations of Western Europe. Numbers favored the East: the Western powers concentrated on using technology to counter the numerically more powerful communist forces.

The biggest threat came from the tens of thousands of Warsaw Pact tanks poised just over the inner German border. The development of the missile-armed attack helicopter was one measure which promised to counter the armored threat, but although it had many advantages as a potential tank-killer, the helicopter was also potentially vulnerable.

Fighting against a lightly armed insurgent enemy was one thing, but any future European battle was likely to prove too dangerous for the Cobra. Soviet armored forces were invariably shielded by a multi-layered network of antiaircraft artillery and surface-to-air missiles able to engage the relatively slow-moving and vulnerable helicopters at short, medium, and long ranges.

A tougher, more heavily armed machine was required, but until it was available the AH-1 would have to plug the gap. Clearly, if the Cobra was to succeed, its crews would have to develop a whole new way of fighting, at very low level and using every advantage of terrain to mask themselves from hostile fire.

The Army had initiated the AAFSS program to develop the Lockheed AH-56 Cheyenne for the antitank gunship role, but development of the Cheyenne was plagued by problems. Both Sikorsky and Bell recognized the Army's problems, and both companies made unsolicited approaches to the Pentagon to plug the gap.

Sikorsky offered the S-67 Blackhawk, a new, dedicated gunship design that bore no relation to the later S-70 Black Hawk utility helicopter. Bell used its experience with the Cobra to offer an upgraded refinement of the Model 209, the Model 309 King Cobra.

Bell built two prototypes. One was powered by a Pratt & Whitney Canada T400-CP-400 Twinpac engine, much like that used on the AH-1J. The second was powered by a single Lycoming T55-L-7C turboshaft engine able to deliver 2,000hp (1,470kW).

The Twin King Cobra first flew on September 10, 1971. Similar in general appearance to the AH-1J, it had a distinctive "buzzard beak" nose and a ventral fin. However, it was not a rebuilt AH-1J, and it incorporated significant changes. The airframe was strengthened and the tail boom was lengthened. A new, longer rotor with forward-swept tips was fitted, giving improved lift and reduced noise. The King Cobra carried a large 20mm ammunition tank derived from the ammunition drum fitted to the General Dynamics F-111 Aardvark bomber, which necessitated the deepening of the helicopter's fuselage.

Sensors were upgraded to give the King Cobra enhanced all-weather ability. The SMS was based on systems developed for the AH-56 Cheyenne, and incorporated a Forward-looking Infrared (FLIR) system, a Low Light TV (LLTV), a laser rangefinder, and a missile guidance system. The SMS could display imagery on either the gunner's sight or the pilot's HUD. The pilot had a separate LLTV system to enable him to control the helicopter while the gunner concentrated on finding targets. The pilot's LLTV sensors were mounted in the front of the rotor fairing. Advanced new avionics were fitted. The Litton Inertial Navigation System (INS) was computerized, and could store 16 different pre-programmed navigation waypoints and worked in conjunction with a radar altimeter fitted with a ground warning system for operations in low visibility.

The primary weapon of the King Cobra was to be the new wire-guided BGM-71 TOW antitank missile, which had proven highly effective in 1972 combat test firings in Vietnam from UH-1 Huey gunships. This weapon could be carried in a pack of four missiles, with one pack under each stub wing. Both the gunner and the pilot had Sperry Univac helmet-mounted sights

A major part of the Sea Cobra's mission for the Marine Corps is to provide the closest of close support for amphibious operations. Deploying from assault ships just offshore, they are among the first support assets available to the troops on the beaches. (US Marine Corps via Aerospace/Art-Tech)

to allow them to acquire targets for the King Cobra's missiles and gun.

The single-engine King Cobra first flew in January 1972. Other than engine fit, it was almost identical to the twin-engine King Cobra. However, it was wrecked in an accident in April, and to complete the US Army evaluation the twin-engine King Cobra was modified to the single-engine configuration.

In the spring of 1972, the Army began a competitive evaluation of the King Cobra, the Cheyenne, and the Blackhawk. Unfortunately for Bell, Sikorsky, and Lockheed, in August of that year the Army declared that none of the helicopters met its requirement, and all were rejected.

Model 409 Advanced Attack Helicopter

The Army's rejection of the competing models, although coming as a shock to the rival manufacturers, can be simply explained. Experience in Vietnam and the changing face of military technology meant that the Army needed a drastic re-evaluation of its gunship requirements. The AAFSS program had possibly been too ambitious for the technology of the time, and in any case political interference meant that it had become almost impossible to proceed along that route.

Almost immediately, however, the Army established a new Advanced Attack Helicopter or AAH program, which would run alongside a program for a new utility helicopter. The two new machines were to be powered by twin General Electric T700 turboshaft engines, each delivering 1,500hp (1,103kW), which promised a major increase in performance over existing types.

The specification called for the new attack helicopter to be armed with a powerful 30mm cannon. Its primary antitank armament would be provided by a maximum of 16 TOW missiles, though armament specification was later modified to take into account the development of the AGM Hellfire missile then getting under way. Hellfire, a laser-guided fire-and-forget tank destroyer, promised to be faster and more accurate than TOW, with a greater range and a much more lethal warhead.

Perhaps the most important aspect of the AAH was that it was intended to be able to fight in the most hostile of battlefield environments. Crew and essential systems were to be protected by armor, and the aircraft was to be optimized for combat during NOE operations.

Boeing-Vertol, Bell, Hughes, Lockheed, and Sikorsky all submitted proposals for the AAH program. In June 1973, Bell and Hughes were selected as finalists, and were awarded contracts for the construction of two prototype aircraft. The Bell Model 409, given the military designation YAH-63, was obviously influenced by the company's Cobra experience, but it was far more than an improved Model 209. It featured wheeled

A competent design, the Bell Model 409 lost out in the US Army's Advanced Attack Helicopter competition to the AH-64 Apache. Several senior officers did not like the two-rotor design, and doubts were expressed about the stability of the tricycle landing gear. (Bell Helicopter)

The AH-1T was a significant Sea Cobra upgrade. Apart from more power and a lengthened tail boom, it was the first Marine Cobra to be able to fire TOW missiles. The TOW missile targeting system was fitted in the helicopter's nose. (TRH Pictures)

tricycle landing gear, flat canopy window plates, a T-tail, a large ventral fin, and a three-barreled General Electric XM188 30mm cannon. Because of the low-level requirement, Bell reversed the AH-1's crew positions since it was felt that having the pilot in the front seat would increase safety in NOE flight.

The prototype YAH-63 made its first flight on October 1, 1975. When it crashed nine months later, it was replaced by a static test prototype that was brought up to flight standard.

In 1976 the YAH-63 was ranged against the Hughes Model 77, designated YAH-64, in a competitive flyoff. At the end of the year the Hughes design was declared the winner of the contest, and was to go into production as the AH-64 Apache. Among other reasons, the Army rejected the Bell design because it was felt that the YAH-63's two-blade rotor was more vulnerable to damage than the Apache's four-bladed system.

AH-1T

The loss of the AAH contract did not mean that Bell was no longer involved in attack helicopter production. Manufacture and upgrading of Army Cobras continued, and the Marine Corps expressed a need for greater load-carrying capability in high-temperature conditions. To meet the Marine Corps' requirements, Bell used some of the systems developed for the Model 309 King Cobra to produce an upgraded version of the twin-engine Sea Cobra. The subsequent Marine version of the King Cobra was designated as the AH-1T.

The AH-1T upgrade had the extended tail boom and fuselage and the upgraded transmission and engines developed for the Model 309. Bell took into account a decade's worth of experience with the Cobra in the new design, and priority was given to making the AH-1T more reliable and easier to maintain under field conditions. Additionally, the AH-1T was given full TOW capability, which made the new Sea Cobra a potent antiarmor platform.

Additional missions flown by the AH-1T included direct air support, antitank, armed escort, and air-to-air combat. The TOW missile targeting system used a TSU that could traverse through 110 degrees, and which had an elevation from –60 degrees to +30 degrees. A laser augmented tracking capability, thermal sights and a FLIR made target acquisition and the launch and tracking of all types of TOW missiles possible in most weather conditions. The Cobra was also equipped with a digital ballistic computer, a HUD, and Doppler navigation system.

As with previous Cobra types, external stores were mounted on a pair of external stores points under each stub wing. A representative mix when targeting enemy armored targets would include eight TOW missiles, two 2.75in rocket pods, and 750×20mm rounds. The cockpit was armored to withstand small arms fire, and the composite blades and tail boom were strong enough to cope with damage from 23mm cannon hits.

Bell's gaudily painted prototype of the AH-1W Super Cobra would not have led to any production had Congress not blocked Marine Corps acquisition of the AH-64 Apache. However, the politicians did fund the Whiskey Cobra modification program, which would be applied to the AH-1T inventory. (Bell Helicopter via Aerospace/Art-Tech)

An improved version of the AH-1T, known as the AH-1T+, was proposed to the Shah of Iran at the end of the 1970s. This would have incorporated more powerful T700-GE-700 engines and the transmission of the Bell Model 214ST, and offered a 75 percent increase in power over the International AH-1J then in service. More advanced avionics were also featured, but the overthrow of the Shah meant that the sale fell through. Nevertheless, Bell continued development, and a prototype was flown in April 1980.

AH-1W Super Cobra

By the early 1980s, the USMC aircraft inventory was declining due to attrition, and the Corps sought a fully navalized helicopter to replace its aging airframes. It is no secret that the Marines would have preferred to acquire the AH-64 Apache as their next attack helicopter rather than yet another updated version of the Cobra, but in 1981 Congress refused to release any funds for the acquisition of the Hughes machine. Driven by necessity, the Marines contracted Bell to develop an AH-1T with increased power.

Bell modified the AH-1T+ prototype by fitting the T700-GE-401 powerpack used by the Sikorsky SH-60 Seahawk. Further modifications included fitting prominent exhaust suppressors, the relocation of some of the TOW electronics from the tail boom to prominent cheek fairings, and modifying the fire-control systems to allow the carriage and use of Hellfire and Sidewinder missiles.

Congress allowed the Marine Corps funds to acquire the new machine, which was given the designation AH-1W. The initial order for 44 aircraft plus a single TAH-1W trainer was followed by orders for a further 40 aircraft to be delivered in the early 1990s, and plans were set in motion to convert remaining AH-1Ts to AH-1W standard.

The AH-1W Super Cobra is a day/night marginal weather attack helicopter that provides en route escort for assault helicopters and their embarked forces. It entered service as the only Western attack helicopter with a proven air-to-air and anti-radar missile capability. The primary mission of the AH-1W is as an armed tactical helicopter capable of close air support, low-altitude and high-speed flight, target search and acquisition, reconnaissance by fire, multiple weapons fire support, troop helicopter support, and point target attack of threatening armor. The AH-1W provides fire support and fire support coordination to a landing force during amphibious assaults and subsequent operations ashore.

The AH-1W is an all-weather aircraft, able to fly and fight by day or by night. The Night Targeting System (NTS) in the nose incorporates a FLIR sensor, CCD TV sensor and a Laser Designator/Rangefinder. The NTS is a modification of the existing M-65 TOW fire-control system. (Bell Helicopter via Aerospace/Art-Tech)

The AH-1W retains the basic Cobra characteristics. It is a two-seat twin-engine helicopter capable of land- or sea-based operations. As with all Cobras and most other dedicated gunship helicopters, the rear-seat pilot is responsible for flying the aircraft, while the front-seat pilot controls the aircraft's weapons systems.

The increased power of the T700-GE-401 engines gives the AH-1W better single-engine performance, and increases the helicopter's ability to operate in high-altitude hot environments.

The Super Cobra is armed with a 20mm turret gun, and can carry TOW or Hellfire antitank missiles, Sidewinder air-to-air missiles, Sidearm anti-radar missiles, and a variety of pods for 5in or 2.75in rockets. It has full night-fighting capability with the Night Targeting System (NTS). The NTS further enhanced the AH-1W's warfighting ability by adding a FLIR sensor, Charge-Coupled-Device (CCD) TV sensor, Laser Designator/Rangefinder, Automatic Target Tracking and FLIR, and CCD TV video recording. The NTS is a modification of the existing M65 TOW fire-control system, and provides the AH-1's crew with the ability to detect, acquire, track, lock-on, range, and designate targets by day and night and in all weathers.

Technical evaluation of the NTS took place from May to September 1993; trials were carried out by test squadron VX-5 at the Naval Air Warfare Center, Weapons Division, China Lake, as well as at the Yuma Proving Ground, Arizona, at the White Sands Missile Range, New Mexico, in Bridgeport, California, and on amphibious ships at sea.

The NTS upgrade also included a Canopy/Cockpit Modification (CCM), which replaced the existing canopy, nose fairing, and co-pilot/gunner instrument panel to make provisions for the NTS and added the Tactical Navigation System (TNS) to the front cockpit. Additionally, a communication/navigation upgrade, ECP 1686, incorporated an ARC-210(V) Electronic Protection (EP) Radio, an ARN-153 V-4 TACAN, and the fitting of an AN/ASN-163 Embedded Global Positioning System/Inertial Navigation System (EGI) commenced in 1996. The CCM modification has resulted in increased efficiency in the front cockpit and helps divide cockpit workload between the front and rear seats.

A further modification has reduced the Cobra's vulnerability by increasing its electronic countermeasures. The ECP-1674 Electronic Warfare (EW) Suite is designed to alert and protect the aircraft from surface-to-air and air-to-air missiles. The AN/AAR-47 Missile Warning System (MWS) provides visual and audible warnings of missile detection, and automatically initiates countermeasures by activating the AN/ALE-39 Countermeasures Dispenser Set (CDS). An AN/AVR-2 Laser Warning Receiver detects the distinctive pulsed laser light emitted by enemy rangefinders, and provides an audio alert for the crew while classifying the threat by type and location relative to the helicopter. The

An AH-1W assigned to USS *Nassau* (LHA 4) prepares to land on the assault ship's flight deck. Cobras regularly fly security and anti-terrorist patrols whenever a US Navy amphibious force passes through high-risk choke points like the Straits of Gibraltar. (US Navy)

AN/APR-39A(V)2 Radar Detection System is a passive omni-directional detection system that receives and displays information to the pilot concerning the radar environment surrounding the helicopter.

AH-1Z

The AH-1T that was modified to the AH-1T+ demonstrator and AH-1W prototype was later fitted with an advanced composite four-bladed rotor system that provided better performance, less noise, and greater resistance to battle damage. This "Four Bladed Whiskey" (4BW) Cobra did not lead immediately to a production contract, though the Marines were clearly interested in the prospect, and the rotorcraft was returned to Marine service in a normal AH-1W configuration. However, as it had done before in the face of official apathy, Bell used company funds to continue the development of the concept. Eventually, they unveiled the design of the new AH-1Z Super Cobra.

With the end of the Cold War, funds for buying new weapons dried up, and the US armed services increasingly had to make do with upgrade programs to bring their current weapons up to date. In 1996 the Marines, having once again been refused permission to buy the AH-64 Apache, signed a contract with Bell to upgrade 180 AH-1W Super Cobras to the AH-1Z standard.

The AH-1W's antitank capability was given a significant boost when the helicopter was modified to be able to fire the AGM-114 Hellfire laser-guided missile. Much bigger than TOW, Hellfire can destroy any current armored fighting vehicle. (Bell Helicopter via Aerospace/Art-Tech)

Among the new technologies adding capability to the AH-1Z is the Helmet Mounted Sight and Display system manufactured by Thales and known as Top Owl. Intended as an off-the-shelf option to avoid excessive development costs, the system was selected as the winner by every pilot taking part in a comparison testing study in 2001. (US Navy Systems Command)

In July 1998, Bell Helicopter competitively selected Lockheed Martin for development of the AH-1Z Target Sight System (TSS). The TSS provides advanced third-generation thermal image processing, eye-safe laser rangefinding, target designation, and full fire-control integration.

In August 1998, four AH-1Ws were delivered to Bell Helicopter for conversion into AH-1Z test aircraft. In September 1998, engineers completed a highly successful critical design review of the airframe, which featured a state-of-the-art, computer-generated electronic mockup to convey design details. The design review paved the way for manufacturing development. Also in 1998, the program delivered seven AH-1Ws to the Marine Corps, bringing the current aircraft inventory to 201. Additionally, several other improvements for the AH-1W, including night targeting and communications/navigation systems, continued.

The "Zulu Cobra" features a new, quieter, four-blade composite rotor with an automatic folding mechanism to make the helicopter easy to store on ship, a 10,000-hour lifetime, and the ability to survive hits by 23mm projectiles, as well as a new gearbox, transmission, and auxiliary power unit (APU). The new APU is the same as that used on the Sikorsky S-70 Black Hawk helicopter. A four-blade tail rotor is also fitted. Fuel capacity is increased by 200 US gallons (758 liters), and the fuel tanks are filled with inert gas as they are emptied to reduce fire hazard.

Bearingless, composite main rotor systems were successfully tested at Bell in the early 1980s and are now standard on the Bell 430 helicopter. Based on the performance of this remarkable rotor system, the USMC decided to incorporate it in their new AH-1Z helicopter. This unique rotor system provides unprecedented agility, substantially increased speed, a smoother ride, a more stable weapons platform, and excellent reliability. It also reduces crew fatigue and so enhances combat mission effectiveness.

The AH-1Z upgrade also increases stores capability to six wing stations, including two wingtip stations for missiles like the Sidewinder or Sidearm, and four for unguided rocket packs or TOW or Hellfire quad missile launchers.

Cockpit and avionics are upgraded as well. The new cockpit features two multifunction 6 × 8in flat-panel displays for each crewman, secure radio communications, a tactical digital data system, an inertial-navigation system incorporating a GPS receiver, and a digital map display. Both sets of cockpit controls are largely identical, allowing either crewperson to fly the helicopter or fire its weapons. A rudimentary backup cockpit flight-control panel operating off battery power is also provided for each pilot; this is a real necessity in today's electronically controlled aircraft, since any kind of power failure would otherwise completely disable the AH-1Z.

The AH-1Z is equipped with a nose-mounted AN/AAQ-30 "Hawkeye" TSS. This features a FLIR imager, low-level-light color zoom TV, a laser rangefinder, and an eye-safe laser target designator. The new FLIR imager is the key to the TSS. Earlier FLIRs lacked the range to allow combat crews to identify a target from more than a few kilometers

Key to the AH-1Z's all-weather performance is the Hawkeye Target Sight System (TSS). The third-generation FLIR used in the TSS has large-aperture optics and an extremely effective stabilization system, allowing target identification from at least double the range of earlier infrared imaging systems. (US Navy Systems Command)

away, but the third-generation FLIR used in the TSS has large-aperture optics and an extremely effective stabilization system, allowing target identification from beyond the range of the Hellfire missile.

Zulu Cobra flight crews are equipped with advanced flight helmets developed by BAE Systems of the UK, now part of the French Thales concern. One of the core elements of the flight system, the helmet, known as Top Owl, features a high-resolution projection TV that can display flight or targeting data and imagery on the visor. It can be fitted with snap-in low-light cameras to provide a highly integrated night-vision capability. The helmet weighs only 4.8lb (2.2kg) with the cameras in place.

Other system enhancements include a new self-defense suite, airborne target handoff system, an onboard systems monitor, two mission computers, and a mission data loader. The self-defense suite includes four ALE-47 chaff-flare dispensers that can be set to manual, semiautomatic, and fully automatic modes, along with an APR-39A radar warning receiver, an AVR-2 laser-warning unit, and AAR-47 missile warning unit.

First flight of a prototype AH-1Z was in late 2000, with initial remanufacture of operational aircraft beginning in 2003 and last delivery expected in 2013. The Marines plan to use the AH-1Zs at least until 2020. The cost of each rebuilding is $11.5 million, with each upgrade taking 13 months.

During its 2003 testing program, the AH-1Z demonstrated a doubling in payload and a 20 percent increase in range and endurance over

An AH-1Z together with the latest upgrade of the Huey, the UH-1Y, aboard the assault ship USS *Bataan* (LHD-5) off Virginia. During the shipboard compatibility trials, the two helicopters completed nearly 30 flight hours and made 267 landings by day and night. (US Navy Systems Command)

the AH-1W. The digital cockpit enhanced pilot situational awareness and reduced workload in some areas. However, poor targeting performance of the newly installed TSS degraded mission effectiveness and increased pilot workload. Problems with TSS stability, focusing, target loss during field-of-view changes, and anomalous TSS behavior had to be resolved before this aircraft could be considered operationally effective.

One-off Cobras

A small number of one-off Cobra modifications and applications have been developed or proposed.

A single AH-1G was provided to the Langley Flight Center, US National Aeronautics & Space Administration (NASA), where it was painted in the NASA test colors of white with blue detailing. It was used for a variety of experiments. It was later passed on to the NASA Ames Flight Center, where it mostly served as a chase aircraft, and was finally returned to the US Army, where it was updated to the AH-1S configuration.

The US Customs Service obtained a handful of AH-1Gs to help hunt down drug runners operating in fast boats and light aircraft. These helicopters were unarmed, featuring a searchlight instead of weapons in the nose turret, and were referred to as "Snakes."

During the 1980s, the original YAH-1S prototype was modified to become the Model 249 demonstrator for a possible updated Army Cobra. The aircraft had an uprated engine, a four-bladed rotor, and various experimental equipment fits, such as Hellfire missiles. The various configurations of the Model 249 never resulted in a production order, but they did help crystallize ideas that would emerge in the systems applied to later Cobra updates.

One of the configurations of the Model 249 was the PAH-2 Cobra. This was developed to meet a German requirement for an antitank helicopter, a requirement that would eventually result in the development of the Eurocopter Tiger. The PAH-2 had an advanced sensor package, a four-blade rotor, and armament of eight Euromissile HOT antitank missiles. As with the other Model 249 configurations, there were no buyers.

COBRA IN ACTION

AH-1 in Vietnam

The Cobra first went into action in Southeast Asia. Impressed by Colonel George P. Seneff's advocacy of the AH-1, Army Chief of Staff General Johnson sent Seneff to Vietnam as the first commander of the 1st Aviation

AH-1Gs of the 7th Cavalry Squadron, 1st Cavalry Division, undergo morning maintenance at the divisional helicopter base at Vinh Long in October 1969. The Cavalry had begun Cobra operations in the previous year following the end of the Tet Offensive. (US Army)

Brigade. The AH-1G arrived at Bien Hoa Air Force Base in South Vietnam in August 1967, and found itself in the thick of combat immediately, being initially employed by the 1st Cavalry Division (Airmobile).

Huey Cobras were used to escort transport helicopter forces and provide fire support for ground operations. They were also used in conjunction with fast Hughes OH-6A Cayuse scout helicopters in devastatingly effective "hunter killer" or "Pink teams". The OH-6 would fly low and slow in an attempt to find Viet Cong units. If it was fired upon, the Cobras were ready to hit the enemy who had just revealed themselves. AH-1s were also used in other roles when necessity demanded, including armed reconnaissance, target spotting, and even search and rescue. By the end of 1968, there were 337 Cobras in Vietnam.

While many gunship crews liked the speed, agility, and the slender lines of the Cobra, all of which made it harder to hit from the ground, there were others who preferred the old Huey gunships for the job, since the door gunners they carried not only provided additional eyes and ears, but could lay down suppressive fire to the rear of the helicopter.

The Cobra's primary external warloads were seven-round or 19-round 2.75in rocket pods. The rockets were available with a variety of warheads, including high explosive, antipersonnel flechette (known as "nail"), white phosphorus incendiary, and smoke. Four-round 5in Zuni rocket pods were also qualified, but were rarely used. The rocket pods were called "Hog pods" and a Cobra with a full load of four Hog pods was called a "Heavy Hog".

Early Cobras with the one-gun turret sometimes also carried one or two SUU-11/A Minigun pods on the stub wing pylons, with 1,500 rounds per pod. Both rockets and guns had advantages and disadvantages. The Minigun was accurate and had an awesome rate of fire, but its range and killing power were limited. Though the 2.75in rockets had much more reach and punch, they were not very accurate, and had to be fired in salvos designed to blanket a target to ensure a hit.

In 1969 many AH-1Gs were fitted with the XM35 cannon system, which was based on the six-barrel GE M61A1 Vulcan 20mm Gatling gun. It was carried on a pylon, with a streamlined fairing attached to the left side of the helicopter on the top of the landing skid for ammunition storage. Panels were added below the cockpit to provide protection from muzzle blast, but such was the power of the new weapon that, incredibly, crews had to physically hang on to canopy panels when firing to keep them from popping open.

Vietnam's hot and humid climate also caused a number of problems to early Cobra crews. The large expanse of the AH-1's canopy made it an effective greenhouse, and operations under the tropical sun turned the

Cobras and OH-6 Cayuse light observation helicopters worked as "Pink Teams". The small "Loach" would fly low to attract enemy fire, and once the Viet Cong had given away their position by firing, they were engaged by the AH-1's heavy armament. (US Army)

cockpit into an oven. The ventilation blowers fitted to the AH-1G were totally inadequate for service in Vietnam, and a much more effective air-conditioning system – Environmental Control Unit (ECU), in military language – was installed in the field. Later production aircraft were fitted with adequate air conditioning on the assembly line.

Externally, one of the most noticeable changes prompted by operational experience was the switch of the tail rotor from the left to the right side of the helicopter. This was done to improve directional control. Retrofits were made in the field by swapping out the entire tail boom with a replacement unit.

During the North Vietnamese spring offensive of 1972, late in the war, two Cobras were shot down by enemy SA-7 shoulder-launched surface-to-air missiles. In an attempt to mask the heat emissions from the engines onto which the SA-7 homed, some aircraft were fitted with an upturned "sugar bowl" exhaust, which directed the hot exhaust gases upwards and theoretically reduced the helicopter's infrared profile when seen from the ground.

In a further attempt to reduce vulnerability, Cobras were fitted with the AN/ALQ-144 IRCM unit on the engine cowling, just forward of the exhaust. The AN/ALQ-144 is what is known as a "hot brick" jammer. A hot ceramic brick core radiates strongly in the infrared. The core is surrounded by a rotating shutter that turns the infrared output on and off. A heatseeking SAM tries to home in on the hot jammer module, but when it is pulsed "off," the missile loses lock and veers off target.

The AH-1G Cobra was basically a daylight weapon, though it could be used at night in a pinch when supported with illumination flares and searchlights. Being able to fly and fight effectively at night is of great value in a counterinsurgency war, and the Army made some effort to develop a night-capable Cobra. The first attempt involved fitting the Southeast Asia Multisensor Armament Subsystem (SMASH) to the Huey Cobra. This incorporated an Aerojet ElectroSystems AN/AAQ-5 Sighting System Passive Infrared (SSPI) sensor turret in the nose, an early example of what would become known as a FLIR. The SSPI was supplemented by an

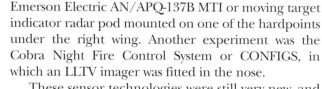

Emerson Electric AN/APQ-137B MTI or moving target indicator radar pod mounted on one of the hardpoints under the right wing. Another experiment was the Cobra Night Fire Control System or CONFIGS, in which an LLTV imager was fitted in the nose.

These sensor technologies were still very new, and neither SMASH nor CONFIGS were successful.

A total of 1,126 AH-1Gs were built, with the last delivered in February 1973. About 300 were lost in Vietnam, with around a third of that number being destroyed in non-combat accidents. Precise numbers of losses are difficult to tally, because in some cases the wrecked Cobras were recovered and rebuilt by enterprising ground crews.

Sea Cobras in Vietnam

After initial training of Marine gunship pilots with the Army, Marine AH-1G Huey Cobras first became operational in Vietnam in April 1969, being flown by VMO-2.

Armorers of the 12th Aviation Company, 1st Aviation Brigade, at Bien Hoa load 20mm cannon rounds into an ammunition canister mounted on the starboard side of an AH-1G. The XM-35 cannon itself was mounted under the port stub wing. (US Army)

A: AH-1G

B

B1: Model D209

B2: AH-1J

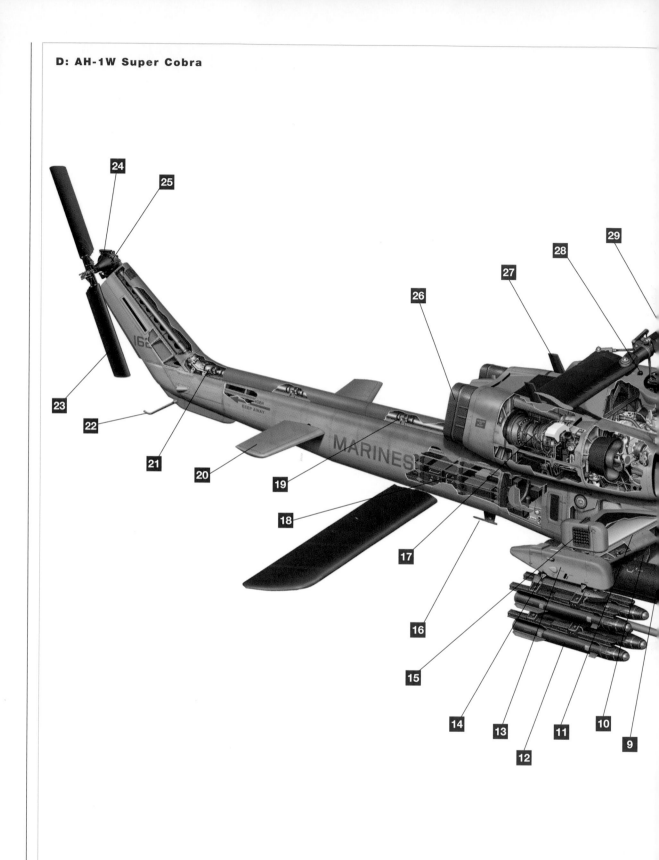

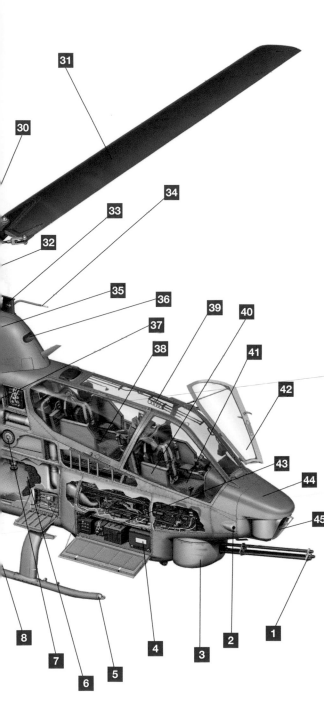

KEY

1. M197 three-barrel 20mm gun
2. AN/APR-44 radar warning receiver
3. M97A1 Universal Turret
4. Ammunition storage bay
5. Landing skid
6. Self-sealing fuel tank
7. Refueling connection
8. Engine air intake
9. 19-tube Hydra-70 2.75in rocket pod
10. Inboard ejector rack
11. Stub wing
12. Four AGM-114 Hellfire missiles
13. Outboard ejector rack
14. ADU-299 pylon adapter
15. AN/ALE-39 chaff/flare dispenser
16. IFF/FM radio antenna
17. General Electric T700-GE-401 turboshaft engine
18. Tail boom frame and stringer construction
19. Tail rotor transmission shaft
20. All-moving tailplane
21. Bevel drive gearbox
22. Tail skid
23. Tail rotor
24. GPS (Global Positioning System) antenna
25. Right angle gearbox
26. Infrared suppression exhaust nozzle
27. AN/ARC-114A FM homing antenna
28. Anti-collision light
29. Two-bladed semi-rigid, teetering rotor system
30. Main rotor mast
31. Main all-metal rotor blade
32. Blade pitch control rods
33. IFF/FM radio antenna
34. Pitot tube
35. Main gearbox
36. Fresh air intake
37. Rotor brake master cylinder housing
38. Pilot seat
39. Cockpit canopy
40. Kevlar armor
41. Co-pilot/gunner cockpit
42. Front cockpit access
43. Avionics equipment in cheek bulge
44. Nose Fairing
45. NTS (Night Targeting System)

AIM-9 Sidewinder missile

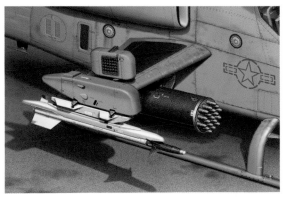

F: AH-1W in Iraq

F

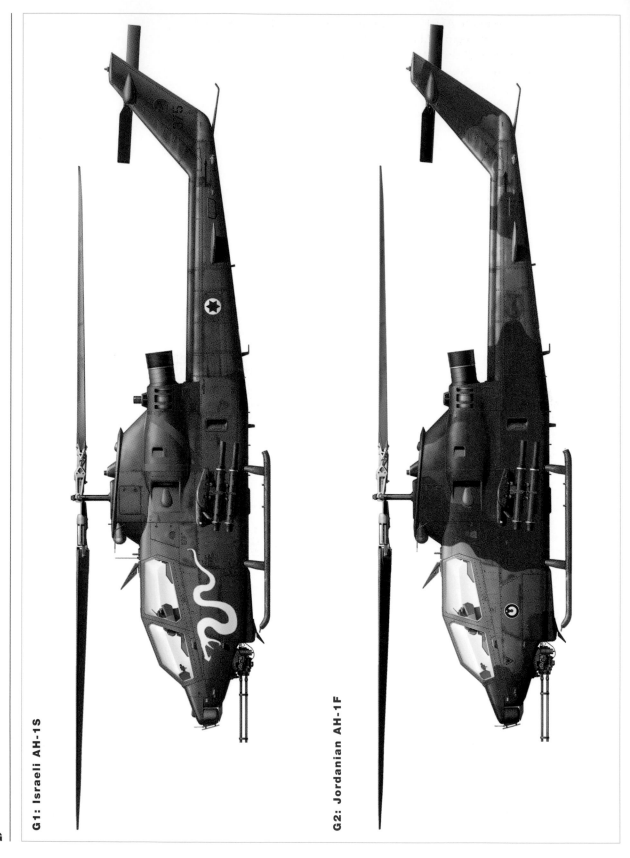

G

G1: Israeli AH-1S

G2: Jordanian AH-1F

In December of that year the AH-1Gs were transferred to HML-367. At the same time, the new twin-engine AH-1J had begun flight testing, and the first four examples reached combat units in February 1971 for a two-month combat evaluation. They were used in action for the first time in March of that year. They participated in the South Vietnamese invasion of Laos, which lasted until April. Having completed their evaluation successfully, the four Sea Cobras were withdrawn.

Operational AH-1Js were deployed to Vietnam from Okinawa during the North Vietnamese offensive of 1972. As with other Cobras, the twin-engine Marine variant was designed as an armed escort for military vehicles, troop-carrying helicopters, and ships, but in Vietnam it was used in a more offensive role. Flying from amphibious assault ships off the North Vietnamese coast, the Sea Cobras flew missions against supplies being offloaded from Chinese and Russian merchant ships in North Vietnamese ports as well as being used to attack antiaircraft emplacements and truck convoys. During the Christmas Linebacker bombing campaign of 1972, the Marine Cobras were used to great effect in suppressing North Vietnamese coastal air defenses.

With the arrival of the twin-engine AH-1J, the Marine AH-1Gs acquired from the Army were eventually passed to a reserve helicopter attack squadron.

Post-Vietnam combat

The United States became slightly isolationist, in a military sense, during the post-Vietnam "hangover" through the second half of the 1970s. The Carter administration was unwilling to engage in military interventions overseas. However, when Ronald Reagan came to power in the 1980s the new President was much more willing to project power in support of his government's policies. Power-projection politics became even more important after the collapse of the USSR, and the Cobra saw action in a number of theaters through the 1980s and 1990s.

Both Army and Marine Corps Cobras took part in Operation *Urgent Fury*, the 1983 invasion of the Caribbean island of Grenada. AH-1s flew close-support and helicopter escort missions. Two Marine AH-1Ts were shot down and three crewmen killed in the action.

The US Army deployed over 140 AH-1 helicopters to Saudi Arabia for *Desert Shield/Desert Storm*, but their performance was overshadowed by the success of the newer McDonnell Douglas (now Boeing) AH-64 Apache. (Associated Press via Aerospace/Art-Tech)

Iranian AH-1Js were in action during the Iran–Iraq War (1980–88), and there are some reports that they engaged in air-to-air combat with Iraqi Mil Mi-24 Hinds. However, the US embargo on exports to Iran ensured that attrition losses could not be replaced, and lack of spare parts meant that by the end of the war most of the surviving Iranian Cobras were grounded.

US Marine Cobras participated in the Persian Gulf escort operations in the late 1980s, when the war between Iran and Iraq spilled over into neutral waters, threatening a large part of the world's oil supplies. Cobras sank three Iranian patrol boats while losing a single AH-1T to Iranian antiaircraft fire.

On December 20, 1989, Cobras took part in Operation *Just Cause*, the US invasion of Panama that overthrew the government of General Manuel Noriega. Five US Army task groups were deployed for the operation, launched from US bases within the Panama Canal Zone, and Cobras provided fire support. Cobra pilots were the first US Army aviators to use night-vision goggles in combat and particularly during the key battle for the Cerro Tigre Panamanian Army barracks.

In 1990, when US and other nationals had to be evacuated from Liberia, the operation descended into chaos and Marine Cobras from the assault ship USS *Saipan* provided overhead protection to the ground units helping with the evacuation.

US Cobras were kept busy in the numerous peacekeeping operations that took place through the 1990s. In 1993 and 1994, Army and Marine Cobras provided support for Operation *Restore Hope*, the US humanitarian intervention in Somalia. They were also employed during Operation *Uphold Democracy*, the US intervention in Haiti in 1994.

Marine Cobras operating off assault ships were used in US military interventions in the former Yugoslavia in the 1990s, and they assisted in the rescue of US Air Force Captain Scott O'Grady in June 1995, after his F-16 was shot down by Serbian air defenses.

Gulf War

Both Army and Marine Cobras were major participants in the Gulf War in 1990–91. The Marines committed 91 Cobras, while the Army brought in 140. Operating from forward, dispersed sites in the desert, Cobras destroyed hundreds of Iraqi armored vehicles and other targets in the fighting, though the Army used its more formidable AH-64 Apaches for the most aggressive gunship assaults. No Cobras were shot down by the Iraqis, though two were lost in accidents during the fighting and a third after the fighting.

Two US Marine AH-1W Super Cobra helicopters from the 26th Marine Expeditionary Unit fly over the live-fire range at Glamoc, Bosnia and Herzegovina, on April 2, 1998. The Marines are assigned to the Strategic Reserve Force of the Stabilization Force (SFOR) keeping the peace in the volatile region. (US Department of Defense)

The Marine Corps deployed four of six active force squadrons to Southwest Asia during Operation *Desert Shield/Desert Storm*. The deployment required no additional augmentation to squadron support personnel and only one Bell Helicopter technical representative. During Operation *Desert Storm*, the AH-1W comprised less than 20 percent of the attack helicopter force deployed, yet flew more than 50 percent of the total attack force flight hours. This record was maintained under some of the most adverse environmental conditions ever encountered in modern, high-technology warfare. Temperatures consistently reached the 135–145°F (57–63°C) range. A mix of fine sand and dust, which had the consistency of talcum powder, was a constant threat to man and machine, without considering the effects of the sooty smoke from burning oil wells. Nevertheless, Super Cobras flew more than three times the number of hours per aircraft per month than any other attack helicopter. During the 100 hours of the land campaign, Marine AH-1Ws maintained a 92 percent mission readiness rate and destroyed 97 tanks, 104 armored personnel carriers and vehicles, 16 bunkers, and two antiaircraft artillery sites.

AH-1s deployed regularly to the Middle East through the 1980s, most notably as part of the huge *Bright Star* series of exercises in Egypt. That desert experience was to come in very useful in 1991, when the Cobra went to war in the Gulf. (US Department of Defense via Aerospace/Art-Tech)

Afghanistan

The retirement of the US Army Cobra force was complete by 2001, so the Marine Whiskey Cobras that have continued in combat operations in the 21st century have done so on their own. They participated in the later stages of Operation *Enduring Freedom*, the American intervention in Afghanistan in 2001–2002. In November 2001 Cobras operating off USS *Peleliu* escorted CH-53E transport helicopters moving a Marine force to Camp Rhino, a forward operating base west of Kandahar. After operating with US Navy fighters to fight off Taleban ground attacks, the Cobras moved to Kandahar airport.

In March 2002, five Cobras of HMM-165 took part in Operation *Anaconda*, the major US effort to destroy a large pocket of Taleban and Al Qaeda fighters in the Shah-I-Kot valley of eastern Afghanistan. In the course of 200+ *Anaconda* missions, the five AH-1Ws fired 28 TOWs, 42 Hellfires, 450 70mm rockets, and 9,300 rounds of 20mm ammunition.

Iraq War

The next major mission for the Cobras came early in 2003 with Operation *Iraqi Freedom*, the invasion of Iraq. The aircraft that Marine crews flew were essentially the same as they had flown in the Gulf War 12 years before, but the war they fought, and the occupation duties they assumed after the capture of Baghdad, were very different.

Marine Light Helicopter Attack Squadron HML/A 269 Gunrunners was based at New River, North Carolina, in late 2002 when it received orders to prepare for combat in Iraq. The unit had been reinforced to a strength of 18 AH-1Ws and nine UH-1Ns when it embarked on the assault ships USS *Saipan* and USS *Ponce* in January.

A ground crewman from Marine Light Attack Helicopter Squadron 773 removes a jammed M89 feeder from the 20mm nose cannon of an AH-1W Super Cobra. The squadron was located at Forward Operating Base Salerno, Afghanistan, in the summer of 2004. (US Marine Corps)

It took ten days to cross the Atlantic, during which time the Cobras practiced shipboard operations. To protect against possible terrorist attack, there were at least six fully armed Cobras in flight when the amphibious force passed through the maritime choke points of the Straits of Gibraltar, the Suez Canal, and the Straits of Hormuz. By the middle of February 2003, the Cobras were ashore in Kuwait, joining Marine Air Group 39 under the command of Marine Air Wing 3 (MAW 3). Marine Air Group 29, normally based in California, also deployed to Kuwait, giving MAW 3 a total force of some 54 AH-1Ws deployed in three reinforced squadrons.

On March 21, three US armored formations pushed forward into Iraq. The US Army 3d Infantry Division was to the west following Iraqi Route 8, the 5th and 7th Marine Divisions attacked through the center along Route 1, while the 1st Marine Division provided the eastern prong of the attack advancing along Route 7.

A Forward Air Refueling Point known as FARP Riverfront was established at Jalibah, which became home to the Marine maintenance teams. From there the AH-1Ws flew 31 sorties on the first day of the war, supporting a Marine ground drive to capture the Rumaylah oilfields. On March 22, a number of Cobras were detached to support British forces in the capture of Basra airport.

On March 23, the Cobras were heavily involved in the fierce fighting for An Nasiriyah. Marine armor became stuck in the boggy ground, and several Cobras were damaged by 37mm and 57mm antiaircraft fire. However, none of the aircraft were shot down. In fact, although 44 of 54 Cobras involved in the active stages of the war were damaged, only two were lost, providing ample proof of the inherent strength of the AH-1's airframe. One Cobra rotor blade took a direct hit from a 23mm shell, blowing a baseball-sized hole in the leading edge, but the crew remained in action for another four hours before returning 40 miles (64km) to their forward operating base.

The Cobra's combat record is in marked contrast to the experience of the Army's Apache squadrons, which suffered more severely than the Marines in spite of the fact that their AH-64s were better protected and had more advanced systems.

At Karbala on March 23/24, 32 Army Apaches suffered a particularly bloody nose when they stumbled into an Iraqi trap. In a deep-strike mission the Apaches unexpectedly ran into the same kind of opposition as the Marines had faced at An Nasiriyah. Most of the helicopters involved were badly shot up and two were lost. There were no serious injuries to the crews, a testimony to the good protection provided by the type, but the incident did enhance the Marines' view of the Cobras' comparative abilities, despite their constant previous desire for Apaches. After Karbala, the Marines could see that their Cobras weren't such a compromise after all, though the Karbala fiasco was generally attributed to unimaginative tactics and not any inherent flaw in the AH-64.

Even before arriving in Iraq, the Marines had decided that they were never going to hover over the battlefield. Using tactics that dated back to Vietnam, they attacked on the move. Running in fast, they would make a single firing pass and then get away. Any further attacks were made from different directions. Pilots never attacked at speeds of less than 70 knots (80mph), since training experience had shown that such a speed made it difficult for a gunner to track a low-flying target.

In the event, 70 knots proved to be too slow, so the Marines were quick to revise their tactics and flew at even faster speeds over exposed terrain. The Army's OH-58D Kiowa Warrior pilots had a similar approach, one commenting that "You'll never catch me hovering. If you want to stay alive, you've got to keep on moving, and the faster, the better."

Unfortunately, the Army's Apache battle drills were less flexible, emphasizing hovering out of the range of enemy ground fire and engaging with long-range missiles before closing in with guns and rockets. The Iraqi trap at Karbala saw the Apache force engaged by enemies who had remained hidden until they opened fire. The end result was that Apaches mounted no more major missions until the Iraqi surrender.

Over the next weeks the tempo of operations for the Cobra units became ever more intense. At the end of March the Marines pushed through the remnants of the Iraqi 14th Division retreating from An Nasiriyah, and prepared for a major fight with an Iraqi Republican Guard division south of Baghdad. Each of the Whiskey Cobra squadrons maintained four two-ship flights in the air each day to cover the advance, with three further flights during the night.

The expected resistance from the Republican Guard did not materialize, but as the Marines advanced into Baghdad they encountered more and more opposition from militias and paramilitary forces. Over the next days the Marine helicopters flew large numbers of close air support missions ahead of the advancing ground troops, and continued to do so until Baghdad finally fell on April 12.

The Cobras flew with heavy armament loads, typically including four Hellfires, four TOWs, and 14 2.75in rockets, half with blast-fragmentation

December 28, 2001. Marines aboard a Light Armored Vehicle (LAV) prepare to go on patrol from the Marine Corps Base in Kandahar, Afghanistan, during Operation *Enduring Freedom*. An AH-1W Super Cobra flies by, on call for immediate fire support if necessary. (US Navy)

Marine Wing Support Squadron 373 established a Forward Air Refueling Point (FARP) at Tikrit, Saddam Hussein's home town, after its capture in 2003. Members of the unit are seen reloading an AH-1W with Hellfire missiles. (US Marine Corps)

The Arabian Gulf, March 27, 2003. Ordnance technicians aboard the amphibious assault ship USS *Saipan* (LHA 2) inspect live ordnance on an AH-1W Super Cobra before flight operations during Operation *Iraqi Freedom*. (US Navy)

warheads, half with anti-personnel flechette warheads. The Marines were able to use the latest Hellfire variant, the AGM-114N, which had a "thermobaric" warhead, a form of fuel-air explosive (FAE) with a far greater explosive shock than traditional FAEs. Antiarmor Hellfires tended to go right through buildings without causing much damage, while Hellfires with blast-fragmentation warheads did not have the punch to destroy larger buildings. The AGM-114N, however, did have the "kick," one Marine saying that he shot one at a big building to take out a sniper "and the whole building collapsed."

There were complaints that the M197 cannon jammed much too often, which apparently has been a long-standing problem, but overall the Marines were impressed by the survivability of the Cobra.

The conflict in Iraq was a severe test for the Cobra nearly four decades after it first entered service, and it also tested the current Marine warfighting doctrine. However, both gunship and tactics came through with flying colors. The Marines have been trained to fight on a fast and fluid battlefield that contains a mix of hard targets and fast-moving soft targets, many of which would appear unexpectedly to threaten the advancing ground forces. Such attacks require immediate action from the escorting helicopters, and the Cobra, despite its age, proved more than equal to the task.

Since the end of the combat phase of the war, Marine Cobras have continued to support anti-insurgent operations, and have been of immense importance in flying the escort missions for which they had originally been developed back in the 1960s. However, the intensive use of the Cobra has not been without cost. According to General Robert Magnus, deputy Marine commandant for programs and resources, there are simply not enough of them in service.

Since the end of the main combat phase of operations in Iraq, Cobras and a small number of unmanned drones have flown overhead surveillance missions, providing cover for ground convoys. They have also supported a number of major offensive operations against insurgent strongholds in the Sunni Triangle west of Baghdad and in villages along the Syrian border.

An escalation of attacks against convoys in recent months has fueled the demand for aerial reconnaissance, and there simply are not enough helicopters or UAVs around. Lieutenant General Michael Hough, deputy commandant for aviation, pointed out a further complication – the Cobra is no longer in production. "We lose one and it's gone, I can't replace it."

FOREIGN COBRA USERS

Although it has been fully replaced by the AH-64 Apache in US Army service, the Cobra remains a frontline weapon with the US Marine Corps and with a number of armies and air forces around the world. The earliest non-US operator was the Spanish Navy. In the early 1970s, Spain purchased eight new-build AH-1Gs, and redesignated the type as the Z-14. These were equipped with the M35 20mm cannon system, and were used to support coastal patrol boats. Four of the Spanish Cobras were lost in accidents, the rest being retired in 1985. Three were sent back to the United States and one was kept in storage in Spain.

Bahrain

Established in 1976, the Bahraini Amiri Air Force (BAAF) expanded in the 1980s. Spurred on by the Gulf War of 1990–91, Bahrain acquired eight AH-1E Cobras and six TAH-1P trainers, delivered in 1994. A further batch of 16 AH-1Es were delivered through to 1997, and the type was operated in two squadrons. The BAAF is now looking to upgrade its force by acquiring up to 17 AH-1Fs.

Iran

In December 1971, Bell signed a contract to deliver 287 Model 214 Huey utility helicopters, and 202 improved AH-1J Cobra gunships to Iran. The improved Cobra, known as the International AH-1J, featured an uprated powerpack and a stronger transmission that could provide up to 1,675hp (1,231kW) continuously. About a third of the AH-1Js delivered to the Shah's forces were TOW capable.

The AH-1Js were used extensively in the Iran–Iraq war, during which as many as 100 aircraft were lost. Cobras fought in a number of the massive land battles of the conflict, and played a key part in stopping a major Iraqi offensive in 1988. Further attrition after the war brought strengths down to around 50 aircraft, and serviceability in the face of a US arms embargo became a major problem. However, Iran by necessity has developed a considerable indigenous maintenance capability, and in recent years the Iran Aircraft Manufacturing Company has even started developing its own upgrades to the Cobra fleet, fitting new avionics and multifunction cockpit displays.

Iran acquired over 200 International AH-1J gunships in the 1970s. After the overthrow of the Shah they were used by the Islamic republic to some effect in the long and bloody war with Saddam Hussein's Iraq. (Bell Helicopter)

Israel

Israel is one of the most experienced users of the Cobra. The need for a gunship became clear after the massed Arab tank attacks of the Yom Kippur War of 1973. The Israelis obtained 12 AH-1Gs in 1977, which at that time were still primarily aerial assault and escort helicopters and which lacked precision antiarmor capability. These, given the Hebrew name of Zefa or Viper, had been upgraded to AH-1Q TOW Cobra standard by the summer of 1978. Further AH-1S helicopters were acquired, and by the time of the Israeli invasion of the Lebanon in 1982 they were operating alongside Hughes 500 Defender scout helicopters with the Northern Squadron at Palmachim. Although the action in the Lebanon was not that for which the Cobras had been acquired, or for which its crews had trained, the squadron flew 62 sorties and launched 72 TOW missiles, claiming the destruction of 51 Syrian targets, including a number of T-62 and T-72 tanks. Two Cobras were believed to have been shot down by Syrian defenses, while a number of others were damaged by ground fire.

More AH-1S Cobras were delivered through the 1980s, allowing a second squadron, the Southern Squadron, to be formed. Further batches of later single-engine Cobra variants have brought the total to at least 40. Most Israeli Cobras have been updated to AH-1F configuration.

Even though the Israeli Defense Forces/Air Force now operates a sizeable contingent of AH-64 Apaches, the Cobras remain an important part of Israel's defenses. They have been used extensively on attacks against targets within the Palestinian Authority, using their TOW missiles to make precision strikes against individual buildings or vehicles.

Israel has further enhanced the lethality of the Cobra with the development of the fiber-optic-guided Spike missile system. The fiber-optic cable connects the missile to the launch platform, relaying seeker imagery to a multifunction display in the cockpit. Guided by the gunner, who can see exactly what the missile sees, it has displayed greater accuracy than any laser-guided weapon. Another missile system thought to be in service, and which has reportedly been used against Palestinian targets, is the Skybow. A small laser-guided missile originally intended to be fired from tanks or self-propelled artillery, it is claimed to be accurate to within 28in (71cm).

Japan
Japan is the only country to have manufactured the Cobra under license. The Japanese Self-Defense Force bought two AH-1Es, one in 1979 and one in 1980, leading to the production of at least 89 AH-1S Step 3 aircraft by Fuji Heavy Industries. Powered by Kawasaki T53-K-703 turboshaft engines, the Step 3 Cobras were roughly equivalent to the US Army's AH-1F. Japan's Cobras serve in five two-squadron units, plus a single training squadron.

Jordan
The Royal Jordanian Air Force recognized a need for some kind of heliborne antiarmor capability in the late 1970s. In 1981, the US government offered to supply TOW Cobras, and 24 AH-1S aircraft were delivered in 1985. Nine ex-US Army AH-1Fs were delivered in 2000 and 2001, to replace losses and to augment the Jordanian Cobra fleet.

Republic of Korea
Following the acquisition of eight International AH-1J Cobras in the late 1970s, South Korea obtained 90 Modernized AH-1S Cobras with C-NITE night-fighting capability. Delivered through the late 1980s and early 1990s, the aircraft were later redesignated as AH-1Fs. Since 1992 Korea has been going through an involved process of replacing the Cobras, but funding problems meant that by 2000 the decision had been postponed, and a new requirement for smaller multipurpose attack scouts was emerging.

Pakistan
Pakistan ordered 20 AH-1S Cobras in the early 1980s, after Bell won a Pakistani Army Aviation Corps competition against the Hughes 500MD. The first batch of ten was delivered in 1984, the remainder arriving in 1986. An option for ten further machines fell foul of the US arms embargo established over Pakistan's nuclear weapons program. When the United States resumed arms sales to Pakistan in the late 1990s, new C-NITE sensors, TOW launchers, and 2.75in rockets were delivered, bringing the Cobras up to AH-1F standard. Further ex-US Army AH-1Fs were ordered in 2004. Since the end of Operation *Enduring Freedom*, Pakistan's two squadrons of Cobras have seen sporadic action against Taleban and Al Qaeda guerrillas on the Pakistan/Afghanistan border.

Nicknamed Zefa, or Viper, the Cobra equips two frontline squadrons with the Israeli Defense Forces. Both the Northern and the Southern Squadrons use a Snake insignia, but on Southern aircraft it is painted larger than on the Northern aircraft seen here. (Private collection)

Taiwan

Taiwan announced an initial requirement for attack helicopters in 1984. Interest in MBB 105s and Hughes 500MDs was dropped when the United States agreed to sell advanced Cobras to Taiwan. In 1992 the Republic of China Army Aviation placed an order for 42 AH-1W Cobras, which had the ability to fire Hellfire missiles. The first of six production lots were delivered in 1993, with deliveries being completed in 1997. In 2003 Taiwan began to evaluate the AH-1Z and the AH-64 Apache for a possible order of up to 75 aircraft.

Thailand

The Royal Thai Army Aviation Division established an attack helicopter requirement in the 1980s, and four AH-1S Cobras ordered in 1986 were delivered in 1990 as AH-1Fs. They were intended to serve as a cadre for future orders for surplus US Army machines, but they remained the only Cobras in service once plans to acquire more were shelved for financial reasons.

Turkey

Turkey bought 24 used AH-1Ps and later purchased at least nine AH-1Ws. Through the 1990s, Turkish Cobras saw a considerable amount of action in the intense but little-publicized campaign against Kurdish insurgent groups along the border with Iran.

On July 21, 2001, the Turkish government announced that the Bell Helicopter King Cobra had been selected as the winner of a competition to meet the Turkish Army's attack-helicopter requirements. Not related to the previous King Cobra, the new aircraft was a variant of the AH-1Z being developed for the US Marine Corps. Along with wheeled landing gear, it was intended that the King Cobra should incorporate significant amounts of Turkish-manufactured equipment.

The initial requirement called for 50 aircraft at a cost of approximately $1.5 billion, with a possible total build of up to 145 aircraft. In addition to Bell, proposals had been received from Augusta, Boeing, Eurocopter, and Kamov. Kamov and Bell Helicopter were short-listed, and whichever was

Japan is the only country to have built the Cobra under license. Modernized and upgraded, as is most weaponry used by Japan's Self Defense Force, the Japanese aircraft are TOW capable, and are roughly equivalent to the late model US Army AH-1F. (Bell Helicopter)

selected would have been the primary subcontractors on the program, with Tusas Aerospace Industries Inc. of Ankara acting as prime contractor. However, the deal was not finalized.

In May 2004, the Turkish government announced that none of the proposals met expectations on price, delivery schedule, contracts terms, and conditions for technical and administrative issues. As a result, any orders based on that competition were canceled and it was decided to ask for new bids for a new project.

The Royal Jordanian Air Force is one of a number of Middle Eastern forces to operate the Cobra. Many Jordanian officials would have liked to buy the Apache, but the Cobra is much cheaper and although old in origin, it remains a most capable attack helicopter. (Private collection)

CONCLUSION

The AH-1 Cobra was the world's first dedicated armed attack helicopter. Fast, heavily armed, and highly maneuverable, the Cobra has proved itself to be a potent fighting machine in all of America's wars since Vietnam and its influential design set the template for all helicopter gunships that followed. Although it is no longer in production – the last new-build AH-1 was completed in the 1990s – it will remain a highly effective warrior into the 21st century, in the shape of the AH-1Z.

For an interim solution to a gunship requirement formulated by the US Army in Vietnam, which made its first flight more than 40 years ago, the Cobra is one of the classic combat aircraft designs. While it may not have the speed or the armor protection of the AH-64 Apache, it also does not have its price tag. With its ability to fire any antiarmor missile in the US inventory, in addition to carrying both antiaircraft and anti-radiation missiles, the AH-1Z is fully capable of meeting all of the Marine Corps' battlefield ground support needs for the foreseeable future.

BIBLIOGRAPHY

Bell, Dana, *Warbirds Illustrated: Air War over Vietnam*, vols 1–4, London, Arms and Armour Press (1983/4)

Bishop, Chris and R. Dorr, *Vietnam Air War Debrief*, London, Aerospace Publishing (1996)

Bishop, Chris (ed.), *Aerospace Encyclopedia of Air Warfare*, London, Aerospace Publishing (1997)

Burnstein, Jonathan, and Jim Laurier, *US Army AH-1 Cobra Units in Vietnam* (Osprey Combat Aircraft Series), Oxford, Osprey Publishing (2003)

Chinnery, Philip, *Vietnam, The Helicopter War*, Annapolis, Maryland, Naval Institute Press (1991)

Drendel, Lou, *Gunslingers in Action*, Warren, Michigan, Squadron/Signal Publications (1974)

Drendel, Lou, *Huey*, Carrollton, Texas, Squadron/Signal Publications (1983)

Dunstan, Simon, *Vietnam Choppers*, London, Osprey Publishing (1988)

Hewson, Robert, "Bell AH-1 Cobra" in *International Air Power Review* (Spring 2004)

Lake, Jon, "Bell's AH-1 Cobra Family" in *World Air Power Journal* (Summer 1992)

Mutza, Wayne, *AH-1 Cobra in Action*, Carrollton, Texas, Squadron/Signal Publications (1998)

Mutza, Wayne, *AH-1 Cobra Walk Around*, Carrollton, Texas, Squadron/Signal Publications (2002)

Peoples, Kenneth, *Bell AH-1 Cobra Variants* (Aerofax Datagraph no.4), UK, Midland Publishing (1988)

Polmar, Norman and Floyd D. Kennedy, *Military Helicopters of the World*, Annapolis, Maryland, Naval Institute Press (1981)

Richardson, Doug, *AH-1 Cobra*, New York, Prentice Hall (1987)

Siuru, William D., *The Huey and Huey Cobra*, Blue Ridge Summit, Pennsylvania, Tab Books (1987)

Stanton, Shelby L., *Vietnam Order of Battle*, New York, Galahad Books (1987)

Verier, Mike, *Bell AH-1 Cobra* (Air Combat Series), London, Osprey Publishing (1989)

Zahn, Randy R., *Snake Pilot: Flying the Cobra Attack Helicopter in Vietnam*, Dulles, Virginia, Potomac Books Inc. (2003)

An AH-1W Super Cobra from the "Golden Eagles" of Marine Medium Helicopter Squadron 162 provides security for the USS *Kearsarge* (LHD 3) Expeditionary Strike Group in the Atlantic Ocean. Still in the frontline 40 years after it entered service, the AH-1 Huey Cobra will continue to serve with distinction well into the 21st century. (US Navy)

COLOR PLATE COMMENTARY

A: AH-1G

Flown by Company C, 2/20th Aerial Rocket Artillery (ARA) at Bu Dop in May 1970, "Romeo One" was a standard AH-1G Cobra with a non-standard color scheme. Originally painted in standard Army Olive Drab (Federal Standard Paint Code FS 34087), the aircraft's tail boom was painted matt black in order to obscure the national markings while the helicopter was being used in the Cambodian invasion of that year. The "ATE" on the radio compartment hatch indicates that it is a replacement scavenged from another aircraft, the letters being from the words UNITED STATES ARMY normally painted on the side. The "Blue Max" insignia beneath the rotor hub was based on Prussia's Pour la Merité, one of the oldest awards for military valor and which was used by ARA units serving with the 1st Cavalry Division.

B1: MODEL D209

The original Cobra design was a private venture by Bell. N209J was a company-funded testbed that used the rotor, drivetrain and tail boom of the UH-1B/C series Huey gunship married to a completely new fuselage. Painted in olive drab, the Model D209 was completed in only seven months. The new attack helicopter, which incorporated features from Bell's earlier Model 207, rolled out on September 2, 1965, and made its first flight on September 7. Flight testing began on September 23, 1965, and it was clear that the Model 209 was significantly better than competing designs from Kaman and Piaseckl. The aircraft was completed with unique retractable landing sklds,

but the marginal performance enhancement provided by such an aerodynamic refinement came at an increased cost and complexity and a reduction in airframe space. Production Cobras would have fixed skids.

B2: AH-1J

The twin-engine AH-1J Sea Cobra entered service with the US Marine Corps in 1972, just in time to fly missions over Vietnam as US involvement wound down. Operational Marine Corps helicopters were finished in USMC Green (Federal Standard Paint Code FS 34097), but after the end of the war they were often painted in Gloss Field Green with high-visibility national markings as seen here. Combat experience over the next two decades was to see the AH-1J carrying a variety of lower-visibility camouflage finishes, including a gray/green scheme using Medium Gray (FS 35237) and USMC Green, and a desert camouflage incorporating USMC Sand (FS 33711). Total Marine Corps procurement of AH-1Js came to 69, with the last new-build example being rolled out in February 1975. The AH-1J and later twin-engine Huey Cobra variants are sometimes referred to as "Twin Cobras".

Early AH-1Gs are easy to identify from the single, short-barreled gun carried in the TAT-102A chin turret and from the prominent landing lights mounted in the tip of the nose. These were later removed, and the single weapon turret was replaced by one mounting two weapons. (Bell Helicopter via Aerospace/Art-Tech)

C: PINK TEAM IN ACTION

During the Vietnam War, the US Cavalry identified types of unit by color. Scouts were designated as the White Section, troop carriers were Blue, and gunships were Red. Hunter-killer teams of Cobras and LOH-6 "Loach" scouts, combining White and Red, were known as "Pink Teams". Pink teams were used to identify and prepare landing zones (LZs) for aero-rifle platoons mounted in UH-1 Hueys. The task of the Cobra in the Pink Team was to escort the scout helicopter as it flew low to mark the landing zone with smoke, engaging enemy positions if the Loach drew any fire. Two more Cobras would usually escort the incoming infantry, using their rockets and guns to "prep" the landing zone by laying down suppressive fire as the lead Hueys began their descent into the LZ.

D: AH-1W SUPER COBRA

The Super Cobra prototype was first flown on November 16, 1983. Production aircraft were redesignated AH-1W. An initial order for 44 and a single TAH-1W trainer was followed by an additional order for 34, and 39 surviving AH-1Ts were upgraded to the AH-1W specification. The AH-1W made its major combat debut in the Gulf War, and it carried several paint schemes. HMLA-367 aircraft were seen in USMC Brown (FS 30117) and USMC Sand (FS 33711), while HMLA-269 helicopters wore Medium Gray (FS 35237) and USMC Sand. More recently, Whiskey Cobras have been covered in a low-visibility gray finish, known variously as Light Ghost Gray or Light Compass Gray (FS 26375) and Dark Ghost Gray or Dark Compass Gray (FS26320).

D: INSET

Originally armed with the BGM-71 TOW wire-guided missile or with 2.75in unguided rockets, the Whiskey Cobra can also fire the larger, faster, and harder-hitting AGM-114 Hellfire antiarmor missile. It is the only combat helicopter that routinely carries air-to-air missiles in the shape of the AIM-9 Sidewinder, seen here positioned alongside an FFAR rocket pod.

E: AH-1F

In 1990 the US Army had more than 1,000 Cobras on strength, but by 2000 the aircraft had all but gone from the inventory. The last Cobras had been replaced in European units by 1996, and the AH-1 had gone from Korea by 1997. Most flyable aircraft were operating with National Guard units, like the AH-1F serving with California's 1/18th Cavalry depicted here. Finished in US Helicopter Drab (FS 34031) – also known as Army Helicopter Green – the Guard helicopters had their Regular Army markings hastily painted over, and National Guard identifiers applied to the tail. By 1991 the Cobra had been withdrawn from Army active service completely, replaced by OH-58A Kiowas and AH-64A Apaches. A number of the surplus aircraft were exported to foreign users, and a handful was transferred to the United States Forest Service.

F: AH-1W IN IRAQ

The Cobra, in the shape of the AH-1W operated by the Marines in both Gulf conflicts, proved that it was far from a cheap, low-capability substitute for more advanced designs. Although outshone by the AH-64 Apache – one of the stars that emerged from the first Gulf War – it was still a highly effective close-support weapon, and its performance was no less competent in the same region 12 years later. The Cobra has been used in all its traditional roles over Iraq, flying as an escort to transport helicopters and ground convoys, providing quick-reaction close support to ground troops ambushed by insurgents, and conducting armed reconnaissance missions into hostile territory in the heart of the dangerous Sunni Triangle west of Baghdad.

The AH-1W prototype was modified by Bell to incorporate an advanced four-blade rotor, which offered significant performance advantages and much reduced noise signatures. Not ordered by the Marines, the "Four Bladed Whiskey" nevertheless was to lead to the definitive AH-1Z. (TRH Pictures)

An AH-1E Cobra takes part in Exercise *Caltrop Force* in 1980. The 'E' model was armed with the powerful long-barreled M197 20mm cannon used by Marine Sea Cobras. It was TOW-capable, but it lacked the fire-control system to be able to fire 2.75in FFAR rockets. (TRH Pictures)

G1: ISRAELI AH-1S

Israel's air force was an early user of the Cobra, with evaluation of the AH-1G beginning in 1975. December 1977 saw the formation of the Shfifon Tzahov (Yellow Viper) squadron, the AH-1 having been given the name Tzefa or Viper in Israeli service. In Israel the helicopters are finished in Brown Drab (FS 30118) with large identification chevrons in Yellow (FS 23655). In keeping with their Israeli name, the active Tzefa squadrons – the Northern Squadron and the Southern Squadron, both based at Palmachim – use a snake motif in their squadron badges and as a highly distinctive fuselage marking. The example depicted here is from the Northern Squadron.

G2: JORDANIAN AH-1F

The Royal Jordanian Air Force took delivery of its first Cobras in 1985, and formed Nos 10 and 12 Squadrons to operate the type. Jordanian AH-1s were finished in a distinctive camouflage color scheme incorporating similar Desert Tan and Desert Brown colors to those used by the Israelis and the Iranians, together with Forest Green and US Army Helicopter Green on the nose and wingtips. Small national insignia appear as Black, White, Green, and Red roundels on the sides of the fuselage beneath the cockpit.

An AH-1G of the 1st Cavalry Division dives down to engage a Viet Cong position. Units designated as Aerial Rocket Artillery were field artillery weapon systems, controlled by artillerymen through artillery fire support channels. They proved to be extremely effective in augmenting and extending the range of the conventional artillery of the airmobile divisions. (US Army via Aerospace/Art-Tech)

INDEX